A New True Book

CHINA

By Karen Jacobsen

Flag of The People's
Republic of China

 CHILDRENS PRESS®
CHICAGO

The land near Guilin in southeast China is a center for agriculture.

PHOTO CREDITS

AP/Wide World Photos—29 (right), 30 (left)

© Cameramann International, Ltd.—35 (3 photos), 37 (right), 39 (right)

Reprinted with permission of *The New Book of Knowledge*, 1996 edition, © Grolier Inc.—5

H. Armstrong Roberts—44 (right); © M. Spector, 11; © Gemignani, 14 (left); © Geopress, 34 (right)

Hillstrom Stock Photos—© Arthur Brown, 8, 20 (2 photos), 26

Historical Pictures Service, Chicago—24, 27

© Emilie Lepthien—38 (left)

Photri—12, 16, 34 (left); © R. Harding, 2; © People's Republic of China, 9 (bottom left), 38 (right)

© Tom Stack & Associates—© Ann & Myron Sutton, Cover Inset, 42 (left); © Mark Newman, 6 (top right)

SuperStock International, Inc.—17 (left), 33; © Manley, Cover; © Kurt Scholz, 9 (right), 17 (right), 23 (center), 37 (left), 39 (left), 42 (right), 43 (center), 44 (left); © George Y. Chan, 13, 15; © Hubertus Kanus, 19 (top); © A. Tessore, 21; © David Forbert, 23 (left and right); © Shuster, 41

Third Coast Stock Source—© Eugene G. Schulz, 6 (top left); © Joe Carini, 6 (bottom left)

TSW/CLICK-Chicago—© D. E. Cox, 6 (bottom right), 9 (top left); © Marcus Brooke, 19 (bottom); © Mathew Neal McVay, 43 (left); © Cary Wilinsky, 43 (right)

UPI/Bettmann Newsphotos—29 (left), 30 (right), 32, 36 (2 photos)

Valan—© Dr. A. Farquhar, 14 (right)

Len W. Meents—maps on 7, 24

Cover—Great Wall

Cover Inset—Kindergarten children at Dongying Village near Shijiazhuang, Hebei

Library of Congress Cataloging-in-Publication Data

Jacobsen, Karen.
    China / by Karen Jacobsen.
        p.   cm.—(A New true book)
    Includes index.
    Summary: An introduction to the history, geography, economy, people, and culture of China, the third largest country in the world.
    ISBN 0-516-01102-2
    1. China—Juvenile literature. [1. China.]
I. Title.
DS706.J32   1990   90-2200
951—dc20   CIP
                                                AC

TABLE OF CONTENTS

THE NATION

China is a large country in eastern Asia. More than one billion people live in China.

The Yellow Sea, the East China Sea, and the South China Sea form China's east and south coasts.

Today, China is called the People's Republic of China. Its government is communist. China's leaders are all members of the Chinese Communist party.

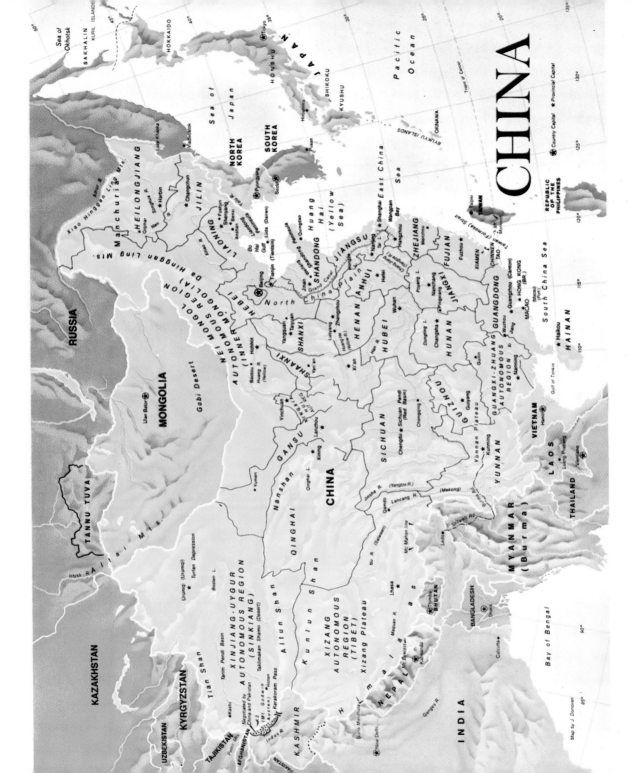

CHINA

⊕ Country Capital   ★ Provincial Capital

REPUBLIC OF THE PHILIPPINES

Sea of Okhotsk

SAKHALIN

KURIL ISLANDS

HOKKAIDO

J A P A N

HONSHU

Sea of Japan

Lake Khanka

Vladivostok

SHIKOKU

KYUSHU

Hiroshima

Tokyo

Yokohama

Pacific Ocean

OKINAWA

RIUKYU (ISLANDS)

Tropic of Cancer

TAIWAN

Taipei

Taiwan (Formosa) Strait

RUSSIA

Amur R.

Xiao Hinggan Ling Mts.

HEILONGJIANG

Harbin

Qiqihar

Songhua R.

Jiamusi

Sungari R.

Da Hinggan Ling Mts.

Manchurian Plain

Changchun

JILIN

Fushun

Shenyang

Jilin

Liao R.

Yalu R.

LIAONING

Anshan

Dalian (Dairen)

Lüda (Dairen)

NORTH KOREA

Pyongyang

SOUTH KOREA

Seoul

Pusan

Huang Hai (Yellow Sea)

NEI MONGGOL AUTONOMOUS REGION (INNER MONGOLIA)

MONGOLIA

Ulan Bator ⊕

Gobi Desert

Altai Mts.

Irtysh R.

TANNU TUVA

KAZAKHSTAN

KYRGYZSTAN

UZBEKISTAN

TAJIKISTAN

Tian Shan

Tarim Pendi Basin

Kashi

Urumqi (Urumchi)

Turfan Depression

Bosten L.

XINJIANG-UYGUR AUTONOMOUS REGION (SINKIANG)

Taklimakan Shamo (Desert)

Hotan

Altun Shan

Nanshan

Qinghai L.

Xining

Lanzhou

Yumen

GANSU

QINGHAI

Negotiated by China and Pakistan

K2 (Mt. Godwin Austen)

Karakoram Pass

AFGHANISTAN

PAKISTAN

KASHMIR

Indus R.

Tarim R.

Kuniun Shan

XIZANG AUTONOMOUS REGION (TIBET)

Xizang Plateau

Lhasa

Maquan R.

Nu R. (Salween)

H i m a l a y a s

NEPAL

Katmandu ⊕

BHUTAN

Thimbu

Ganges R.

Brahmaputra R.

Ganges Delta

INDIA

BANGLADESH

Dhaka ⊕

Calcutta

Bay of Bengal

CHINA

Yinchuan

Baotou

Hohhot

Huang R. (Yellow)

SHAANXI

Yan'an

Xi'an

Yangquan

Taiyuan

SHANXI

HEBEI

Beijing ⊕

North China Plain

Tianjin

Bo Hai (Gulf of Chihli)

Grand Canal

Tangshan

Baoding

Shijiazhuang

Jinan

SHANDONG

Qingdao

Qingdao

Zaozhuang

Huang He (Yellow R.)

Zhengzhou

Luoyang

HENAN

Huai R.

JIANGSU

Grand Canal

Xuzhou

Nanjing

Shanghai

ANHUI

Hefei

Han R.

HUBEI

Wuhan

Yangtze R.

Chang (Yangtze R.)

SICHUAN

Sichuan Pendi (Red Basin)

Chengdu

Chongqing

Jinsha R. (Yangtze R.)

Qamdo

Lancang R.

Mekong

Mt. Meri Irie

Leshan

Salween Rd.

YUNNAN

Yunnan Plateau

Kunming

MYANMAR (Burma)

LAOS

Luang Prabang

Vientiane ⊕

THAILAND

VIETNAM

Hanoi ⊕

Gulf of Tonkin

GUANGXI-ZHUANG AUTONOMOUS REGION

Nanning

Guilin

GUIZHOU

Guiyang

HUNAN

Changsha

Dongting L.

Xiang R.

GUANGDONG

Guangzhou (Canton)

Wuzhou

Xi R.

Zhanjiang

MACAO

Macao

HONG KONG (BR.)

Poyang L.

JIANGXI

Nanchang

Pingxiang

FUJIAN

Fuzhou

XIAMEN

CHINMEN TAO

Wenzhou

ZHEJIANG

Hangzhou

Shaoxing

Wenzhou

Tai L.

Nanjing

Wuhan

Hangzhou

Wangan Bay

East China Sea

South China Sea

HAINAN

Haikou

Map by J. Donovan

Beijing is a bustling, crowded city with many old and new features.

Beijing is the capital city of
the People's Republic. Almost
6 million people live in Beijing.

6

EASTERN CHINA

The eastern half of China is the home of 90 percent of China's people. It has most of China's good farmland and water supply.

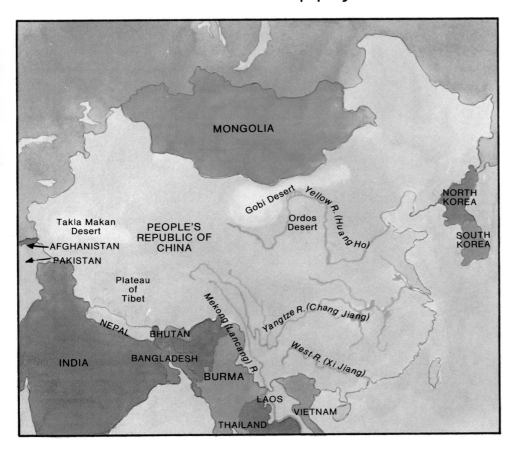

Map showing the rivers and deserts of China

Eastern China has four regions: the Northeast, the Huang Ho River region, the Chang Jiang River region, and the South.

Northeastern China is known as Manchuria. At its center is the Manchurian Plain. The Liao River drains the plain, bringing water to the region's rich farmland.

Wheat is one of the main crops of the farms in northern China.

Chinese industry: a power plant in Gansu Province (above), a steel mill (top left), and an automobile factory (left).

The main city is Shenyang.
The Northeast region produces coal, iron, oil products, motor vehicles, and electricity. Forests cover the mountains to the east of the plain.

The Huang Ho River begins in the Tibetan Plateau and flows almost 3,000 miles to the sea.

In the past, the Huang Ho often overflowed its banks. Today, dams and dikes control the Huang Ho's water.

Farmers in the Huang Ho plain grow sweet potatoes and cotton. Many also raise poultry, pigs, and dairy cows.

The Huang Ho region's major cities are Beijing and Tianjin.

The Chang Jiang
River flows
through rugged
mountains in
eastern China.

The Chang Jiang is
China's longest river. It starts
in the mountains near

Myanmar (Burma) and flows eastward to the East China Sea. The region's water supply, rich soil, and mild climate are perfect for growing rice, China's most important food crop.

Farmers grow rice in fields called paddies, which are flooded with shallow water.

Shanghai is China's most important seaport.

Near the mouth of the
Chang Jiang is Shanghai,
one of the largest cities in
the world. Shanghai has
over seven million people.

Guangzhou (right) is a major center of trade and industry. Lush farmland (above) produces much food in the well-watered southeast.

In the South region, the Xi Jiang River brings water to a fertile plain. Guangzhou (Canton), with almost three million people, is a large port near the Xi Jiang.

On the southern coast of China is the city of Hong Kong. It is a worldwide business center. Hong Kong, a British colony since 1898, will be governed by China after 1997.

Hong Kong is a modern business and trade center with many tall buildings.

WESTERN CHINA

The western half of China
has vast deserts and towering
mountains. Its climate is
harsh—either very dry and
hot or very dry and cold.

In north central China, the
wide Mongolian Plateau is

Huge sand dunes rise along a desert road in western China.

Mongol people (right) live in tents called yurts. They move
from place to place with their herds of horses (left).

the home of wandering
tribes of Mongol people.
Their animals graze on the
plateau's short grasses.

The Gobi Desert straddles
China's border with
Mongolia. In the far west is
the Takla Makan Desert. The

17

Tarim River runs through the Takla Makan. Chinese farmers use the river to irrigate the desert and grow food crops.

Western China has many mineral deposits. There are coal and iron mines near Urumqi and large oilfields near Karamay.

The towering snowcapped mountains of the Tibetan Plateau cover the southern half of the region. The main city in Tibet is Lhasa. It is 12,000 feet above sea level.

The Potala Palace (above) is a landmark in Lhasa,
Tibet's ancient capital. Tibetans (below) speak their
own language and have their own customs.

Archaeologists are digging up an ancient Chinese village (left). The painting (right) shows what the village looked like thousands of years ago.

CHINA LONG AGO

There were people living in China more than 50,000 years ago. They were hunters and gatherers. Thousands of years later, the people in the Huang Ho Valley learned to grow crops and raise animals.

Chinese officials destroying chests of opium brought to China by the British

for tea. The Manchus did not want the opium in their country. There was a war and the Chinese lost.

As time passed, the Manchus lost control of more and more Chinese land to foreign countries.

In 1908, Pu Yi, only three years old, was crowned emperor of China.

SUN YAT-SEN AND THE NATIONALISTS

In 1911, the Chinese rebels in Wuhan started an uprising against the Manchus. The fighting spread and the Manchus were forced to leave China. Pu Yi, the last Manchu emperor, gave up his throne in 1912.

The leader of the uprising was Sun Yat-sen. Sun Yat-sen declared that China was a republic and would have elections for the first time.

Pu Yi (left), the last emperor of China. Sun Yat-sen (right) was a farmer's son from Guangzhou. He was a doctor and had traveled to many parts of the world.

Sun became China's first president. But his government lasted only a few weeks. A powerful general, Yüan Shih-k'ai, took over as president. In 1916, Yüan died, and the republic was finished. In the 1920s, warlords ruled in the north, the west, and parts of south China.

Chiang Kai-shek (left) in 1927. Young Chinese
soldiers fought Chiang's Army (right).

The Nationalists were the
followers of Sun Yat-sen. They
wanted to bring back the
republic. Their army was led
by General Chiang Kai-shek.

The Communists wanted
to completely change China.
They wanted the poor peasants
to own small farms and make
their own laws.

30

The Nationalists and the Communists fought together against the warlords. In 1927, the army captured Shanghai. Then, General Chiang ordered his Nationalist soldiers to attack and kill all the Communists. But many of the Communists escaped. They formed their own "Red Army" to fight Chiang's Nationalists.

In 1931 Japan captured Manchuria. But Chiang didn't fight the Japanese. He kept attacking the Communists.

MAO ZEDONG AND THE LONG MARCH

Mao Zedong in 1937

In 1934, Mao Zedong, the leader of the Communists, decided to march the Red Army to North China. Of the more than 100,000 soldiers who started the 6,000-mile "Long March," only 20,000 survived

In 1937, Japan invaded central China. Chiang and Mao stopped their civil war to fight the Japanese.

COMMUNIST CHINA

Mao Zedong at a Chinese Communist party congress

When the Japanese were defeated in 1945, the war between the Nationalists and the Communists started again. Then, in 1949, the Red Army took over China. China became the Communist People's Republic of China, with Mao as the leader.

33

Fishing in the river (left) and housing for the
people (right) at an agricultural cooperative

In 1950, the government
gave land to China's peasant
farmers. Later, the government
made many small farms
join into groups called
agricultural cooperatives.

The government took over
China's factories and mining
operations. The Communists
tried to control every person,

every activity, and every idea in China.

Mao Zedong died in 1976. The new leaders wanted to make China more modern. In 1982, the government gave the people the right to grow food and make products for their own benefit.

Left: Vegetables for sale in an outdoor market.
Center: A farmer uses an old-fashioned hoe.
Right: Traditional medicines are sold in shops.

Chinese students protesting in Tiananmen Square in Beijing.

In the summer of 1989, thousands of university students gathered in Beijing's Tiananmen Square and demanded more democracy in China. The government sent in troops to stop the protest. Many people were killed.

Both older houses with
thatched roofs (left), and
newer apartments (above)
are found on Chinese farms.

LIFE IN CHINA

More than eighty percent
of the Chinese people live
and work on farms.

Old farmhouses have
stone or brick walls and
roofs made of tile or straw.
Some farm workers live in
new apartment buildings.

Kitchen of a Shanghai apartment (left). Workers in
a steam-turbine factory in Nanking (right)

In China's cities, most
people live in small houses
or apartments. There are
only two or three rooms per
family. Every neighborhood
has its own local government,
called a collective. Most
city people work in factories
and live near their jobs.

Workers in a Chinese restaurant kitchen (left) prepare vegetables for stir-frying. Vegetables are often cut into decorative forms (right).

Chinese food is boiled or quickly stir-fried. In southern China, boiled rice is the most important food.

In China's warm climates, both men and women wear cotton slacks and shirts. In cold climates, people wear many layers of cotton clothing.

EDUCATION

The Chinese government wants everyone to go to school for at least nine years. But there are not enough schools.

At age 7, most children start school. Students use their local language, but they also learn *putonghua*, the official Chinese language. Their other subjects are arithmetic, science, music, art, and physical education.

In the third or fourth grade,

An elementary
school in
Guangzhou

Chinese students begin to study English, Russian, or another foreign language.

Students start junior middle school at age 12. They also spend time learning to work in factories, on farms, and in public places.

At 15, students with good

A kindergarten teacher and student (left). Students in a middle school wire an electric motor (right).

grades go to senior middle school for three years. Graduates may take a test to enter one of China's technical colleges or universities.

The Chinese constitution guarantees religious freedom. But most Chinese are not religious, and the government discourages religious beliefs.

ARTS AND RECREATION

Chinese artists have been painting landscapes for more than 2,000 years. Silk weaving and embroidery are also Chinese arts. The government provides training for actors, dancers, and other performers.

Chinese arts: Opera performers (left), silk embroidery (center), and pottery-making (right)

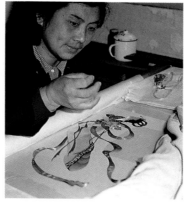

May Day, International Workers' Day, is celebrated with speeches and dancing (left). On New Year's Day (right) lion dancers and drummers parade through the streets.

In early April, the Chinese observe "Qing Ming," or Tomb Sweeping Day. People honor dead relatives by cleaning around their tombstones.

National Day is October 1. China's people celebrate the day in 1949 when Mao Zedong and the Red Army entered Beijing.

Athletic activities are very important. Chinese athletes excel in basketball, soccer, gymnastics, volleyball, and table tennis.

The Chinese people enjoy playing cards, chess, and kite-flying contests.

The people of China have suffered great losses and worked very hard. They have few luxuries. They have done without many things to help make China strong and independent.

WORDS YOU SHOULD KNOW

Asia (AI • zhah) — a large continent east of Europe

bronze (BRAHNZ) — an alloy, or mixture, of the metals tin and copper

capital (KAP • ih • til) — the place where a country's government is located

Chang Jiang (CHANG jee • AHNG) — a river in central China; also called Yangtze River

Chiang Kai-shek (CHANG kye CHEK) — the general who led the Chinese Nationalist Army

climate (KLY • mit) — the usual kind of weather at a specific place

communist (KAHM • yoo • nist) — a form of government under which all the people own all the property and the means of production

democracy (dih • MAH • krih • see) — a form of government under which the people elect their representatives

dike (DYKE) — a wall of earth or other materials built along the banks of a river to control flooding

dynasty (DIE • niss • tee) — a series of rulers from the same family; the time during which members of the same group or family rule a country

Guangzhou (goo • AHNG • jo) — a city on the coast of China; also called Canton

Hsia (shee • AH) — a Chinese tribe; the first rulers of China

Huang Ho (HWAHNG HO) — a river in northern China; also called the Yellow River

independent (in • dih • PEN • dint) — not controlled by others; free of masters

invaders (in • VAY • derz) — armies that come into a country from outside to conquer the country

irrigate (EAR • ih • gate) — to bring water to crops by means of ditches or pipes

Manchuria (man • CHOO • ree • ah) — the northeastern area of
 China
Mao Zedong (MA • oh   TSAY • dong) — the leader of the Chinese
 Communists
opium (OH • pea • yum) — an addictive drug gathered from the
 flower of the poppy
peasant (PEZ • int) — a person who lives on the land and works as
 a farmer
plain (PLAYNE) — a broad flat area of land
plateau (PLA • toh) — an area of elevated flat land
putonghua (poo • TUNG • HWAH) — the official language of China
region (REE • jun) — a division of a country
republic (rih • PUB • lik) — a country whose leaders are elected by
 the people
Sun Yat-sen (SUHN   yat • SEN) — the leader of the Chinese
 Nationalists
technical (TEK • nih • kil) — having to do with science and
 engineering
tribe (TRYBE) — a group of related people
warlord (WAR • lord) — a strong leader who uses military power to
 gain and keep power
Xi Jiang (SHEE   jee • AHNG) — a river in southern China

INDEX

About the Author

Karen Jacobsen is a graduate of the University of Connecticut and Syracuse University. She has been a teacher and is a writer. She likes to find out about interesting subjects and then write about them.